TABLE OF CONTENTS

www.SellBetter.ca

Introduction:
The Reality Of Prospecting and Rejection

Talk to any group of sales people and ask why they don't like prospecting, specifically cold calling, and rejection is at the top of the list. In actual fact, it should say fear of rejection, because all too often they don't even get around to making the calls to be rejected, the fear of it prevents them from picking up the phone to start with. Well here some good news, bad news, and then some real good news.

The first bit of good news is that there is a sure proof way to avoid rejection, don't make the call! And many, as we know have chosen this path as their solution. Unfortunately, and here is the bad news, it leads to anemic or useless pipelines, leading to lean incomes or job loss, and therefore not the ideal solution.

The real good news is that you don't have to fear, avoid or shy away from rejection. In fact if you look at other aspects of your sale, you already know how to deal with rejection. Fact, the average conversion rate for sales accepted leads to actual closed sales is 16.41%.* 6:1 – 1 of every 6 prospects, or an 83.59% rejection rate. The average contact to appointment conversion rate is roughly 14% 7:1, or an average rejection rate of 86%. Not that different, almost 84% of sales you start end up with you and or your value prop being rejected.

Stat derived from two sources: The Long Road from B2B Lead Generation to Sales Conversion – Marketing Sherpa; Sales Benchmark Index

Contrast this with stats I have been collecting from people who successfully adopt our Proactive Prospecting Program, convert one out of every six to eight phone call conversations (yes, cold calls) to appointments. That is 12.5% – 16.6% success rate. About the same as the lead to close. Yet I have never met a sales person who said that they are *afraid of engaging with a buyer or submitting a proposal for fear of rejection.*

For me the key difference is outlook and attitude, specifically rooted in the confidence one gets from a process or methodology. When you have a strategy, a plan, with a corresponding action plan detailed with alternatives and choices based on experience and best practices, execution is more likely and consistent.

Most sales organizations and successful sales people have a sales methodology or process they adhere to and follow in executing their sale. It helps them stay on track and progressively move towards their destination. It gives them options on how to address hurdles or unexpected events and responses from buyers, including how to handle objections throughout the sale, right down to price objections. In essence a detailed road map, with road closures, fuelling stations, and detours. This allows them to cope with challenges along the way, and more importantly put wins and losses in context.

These same organizations do not have a formal process for prospecting, especially prospecting the vast majority of the market, those we refer to as the status quo. Which means there is no step by step methodology, road map, contingencies, and without metrics, no context. If they did they would have some sense of confidence that they are actually executing things correctly, the context to things on track, and how to handle the most common objections. As a result, all they can relate to is the relatively low successes and the seemingly relatively high rejection rate.

But as highlighted above, the real issue is not the rejection levels, but the lack of process, metrics, and context. Without this you don't know if you blew it, or were blown off, all you have is the sense of rejection.

There are various methods out there, once adopted the results speak for themselves, your next step is to pick one that fits with your sale, adopt it, execute, review and refine. Once you do that it will be less about rejection, which you will still experience, and more about understanding, which you can always improve.

The goal of this booklet is not to cover the entire spectrum of the Proactive Prospecting Call, but to look specifically at how to handle the common rejections faced by intrepid sellers. If you are prepared, and can manage the most common objections, you will not only minimize rejection, but engage with more potential buyers, closing more deals, making more money, contribute to society, and who knows, save the planet from whatever you think ails it, knowing whatever it is, it will not be buyer rejection.

Commit to doing it, commit to practicing and improving daily and you will improve you success rate. If along the way you run into challenges, down points, or just feel rejected, I am here to help, just let me know. You can reach me at:

tibor.shanto@sellbetter.ca
+1 416 822-7781
(855) 25-SALES Toll Free
Twitter - @TiborShanto
You Tube – www.youtube.com/sellbetter
LinkedIn – ca.linkedin.com/in/tiborshanto/
Facebook – www.facebook.com/Renbor.Sellbetter

IT'S NOT ABOUT AVOIDING THE OBJECTION – BUT ABOUT HOW YOU HANDLE IT!

CHAPTER ONE

Professional Disruptive Marketing

In the introduction I presented the fact that rejection is not unique to prospecting, we just react differently to it, than when we are rejected at the end of the sale. Funny, but i would much rather be rejected by someone i don't know, never met, that I would not recognize in a coffee line, than by someone I have spent time with and invested energy, emotions and resources into making happy.

As mentioned in the introduction, rather than trying to avoid rejections, sales organizations and sales people need to adopt and adhere to a specific prospecting process, and leverage it for consistent results. The goal is to adopt a method for dealing with rejection, rather than trying to avoid them. With a proper method, executed consistently, you will be in a position to address and manage objections, and convert more of them to conversation and engagement with potential buyers. As an added bonus, with a process you have a means of measuring the outcome, reviewing and adjusting according to a plan.

Dealing with rejection IS part of the process, giving people a methodology for managing objections and leverage them to engage with more prospects. Starting here, that is exactly what you will learn; no matter how you get to the point where the rejection presents itself, you will be in a position to manage them better.

First we will put rejection and objections in context, and then provide ways to manage and use them for success. A combination of a tried and proven best practices used by many leading sales organizations to engage with more of the right prospects. These methods have been gleaned over the years and continue to be refined daily in the field, not only by me, but our clients day in day out, and in the current socially charged recession.

In order to deal with and manage objections, you first need to understand them and put them in context. This is a key point in not only managing objections but overcoming the fear and related call reluctance. The context IS NOT YOU! Let me repeat, the rejection, which will come if you make prospecting calls, is not of you. The context is TIME and VALUE. The demands on the buyer's time, generally greater than the time they have to do all the things they need to. Most people already are trying to pack 16 hours into a 10 hour day, so the last thing they need is a distraction or interruption, no matter how cool your thing might be.

Interruptive Marketing

Let's face it, we are professional interrupters, and that is not a negative it is just a fact, part of our success is based on interrupting people to show them ways they may be able to do what they need to better with our offering. CHANGE DOES NOT HAPPEN WITHOUT AN INTERRUPTION TO THE WAY THINGS ARE NOW. Unless you are on the agenda of the person you are calling, you are interrupting their ability to get through the 16 hours of work they have to finish before they have to get their kids to little league. Given the choice to finish their work - satisfy their boss, or talk to an unknown interruption, guess which wins, leaving us to be rejected.

Now this can be tempered with a structured approach, taking a number of dynamics into account that will help smooth the bumps inherent in an unsolicited prospecting call; and by the introduction of real value into that approach, giving you an opening to change the perception that you are a completely useless interruption, to one of potentially a worthy interruption.

Remember that interruption and disruption are part of the creative process, it causes change, which is what you want, but you need to prepare for the response and deal with it, not surrender and abandon a potential opportunity. As well, injecting a heavy dose of value will only take you from life threatening to critical, meaning you still need to deal with the rejection, but in a more balanced and manageable way.

Let's start by understanding that YOU ARE NOT BEING REJECTED! When you have a proper process and understanding that they are rejecting the interruption, and the collective memory of all the bad interruptions they have lived through in the past, you can act with confidence and gain room to manage and engage. If you can accept that it is not you but the circumstance, it changes the context. Circumstances can be controlled and altered with some forethought and an action plan, you'll find this in the chapters to follow. But it starts here, in you embracing your role as a practitioner of Interruptive Marketing.

Next we'll look at the context VALUE brings, and how to leverage it throughout the prospecting call to achieve the right rejection, yes, the right rejection.

CHANGE DOES NOT HAPPEN WITHOUT AN INTERRUPTION TO THE WAY THINGS ARE NOW.

CHAPTER TWO

Conditioned Response

In the previous chapter I talked about the importance of context when it comes to objections, and a basic understanding of objections at their root. We looked at the importance of context, TIME and VALUE. We looked at how their isn't a right time, just their time and our interruption of it, now let's look at VALUE, and how we can use it to make it easier to manage, handle and leverage them for more engagement.

Understanding that prospects are more rejecting the interruption than you specifically, now let's look at how they deal with those interruption, the nature of the objection. In most instances it is very much a Conditioned Response, they need to react to something effectively, in this case getting rid of us sellers, the interrupters, they find a way that is effective a majority of the time, in fact 80% of the time; and once they do find the way that works to rid them of interruptions, they use it every time and without much thought. Much the way we swat a fly, stop at red lights, look up at a loud noise, all without much thought or effort, it is a Conditioned Response in reaction to a specific occurrence.

Just like when I set out with my wife to buy a new washer, had the specifics thought out, it was just down to picking the retailer. As we were walking in to Sears, talking with my wife about one thing or another, when we were "interrupted" by a very nice rep who asked "May I help you?" Guess what I, and 90% of people who are posed that question say? That's right, "Just looking", a Conditioned Response. Five minutes later, having finished our chat and getting down to business, I looked around, no one in immediate sight, I looked at my wife and complained about the lack of service; even though not five minute before there was a very nice rep offering to help us, and I blew them off without any thought or effort, by saying that I was just looking – a Conditioned Response. Which is exactly what happens when we call a potential prospect unexpectedly, action - reaction. Now consider that I went Sears willingly, looking for a washer, yet I dismissed the rep as they were trying to help me accomplish my objective. I ask you is it possible that the prospects we call, or more specifically, interrupt, are as real with their response?

Again it comes down not to avoiding rejection, but how we handle it. Here is what I mean, let's roll back the film, same store, same wife, same me, same clerk, she again asks the question and I give the same Conditioned Response, but this time she responds and offers up "well if you tell me what you are looking for, I would be happy to show you". Fifteen minutes and a few questions later, I walked out with a washer worth $800, where I had intended to spend only $500.

By handling my objection in a direct, confident and pre-planned way, the clerk was able to take an objection, a rejection, and turn it into a conversation. Further, once I used up my "Conditioned Response", I was left to actually responding to her question directly rather than leaving it to reflex. Which is what you want to do with your prospects, let them use up their Conditioned Response, deal with it, get past the reflex, and begin dealing with the real sales process. Once they have used the conditioned response, subsequent responses will be more real and genuine, not necessarily any more positive, but real, the start of a conversation.

Here is some more good news, 80% of the time they will use the same Conditioned Response, it comes in one of five common objections, that you will from here on think of as five common conditioned responses, in no specific order:

Status Quo
Lack Of Interest
No Time
Bad Experience
Wants to Know More First

Knowing that, as you master dealing with each of these, you will have the ability to deal with and take away 80% of the objections you face, and move closer to a real sales conversation.

Next, the basics of taking away these objections, starting with Status Quo and Lack Of Interest.

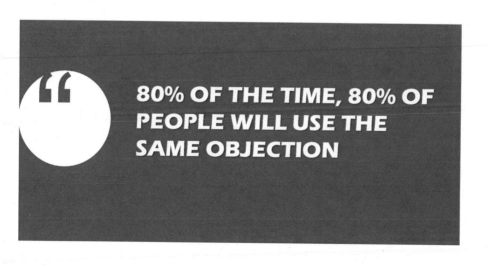

80% OF THE TIME, 80% OF PEOPLE WILL USE THE SAME OBJECTION

CHAPTER THREE

Status Quo & Lack Of Interest

In the first two chapters we looked at the anatomy of the typical objection to a prospecting call that is being an Interruption, and the Conditioned Response to Interruptions. I also told you how 80% of the time you will get one of five common objections:

Status Quo
Lack Of Interest
No Time
Bad Experience
Wants to Know More First

These will come in different flavours, different rhythms, but they will come, and they will be one of these five. So let's see how we can take away these objections, bringing to play the new view of Conditioned Response, and get to having some good meetings in the calendar, and prospects in the pipeline.

While all five have common elements, the Status Quo and Lack Of Interest, are more commonly linked. With all the common objections, and especially with these two, it is as much about dynamics and managing those, than taking on the buyer; remember it is about _handling the objection not the buyer_, if you Take Away the objection, it makes it easier to achieve your objective, which for the prospect to get engaged.

Four step process:

A. Acknowledge – The goal of the exercise is initiate a conversation that for the field rep result in a face to face visit, and for an inside rep a sales call by phone. Conversations take two. When they give their Conditioned Response, address it. One reason people hate the mid-dinner telemarketing call is the one sided nature of the call:

Telemarketer – "if you sign up today…."
Me – "My house is on fire"
Telemarketer – "It will also entitle you for coverage…"
Me – "My daughter's hair is aflame"
Telemarketer – "And if you switch your balance it will be interest free for…"

Address their issue head on!

B. Create Credibility – Different where there is a Lack Of Interest and Status Quo, but the goal is to leverage the momentum of having acknowledged their response, and moving to build credibility.

C. Involve – The credibility above, should also very much involve the prospect, again creating an environment that leads to a conversation.

D. Call to Action – Commitment – Always, I repeat ALWAYS end your response with a call to action, the last thing you want them to do is sit back and analyze your response, remember it is about dynamics and momentum as well as content, again Action - Reaction. You want them to react to your call to action; if you engage them well with the above elements, you want them to think about investing the time.

While approaching both the Status Quo and Lack Of Interest in a similar pattern, there is a key difference between the focus of Create Credibility step. With buyers who are presenting themselves as Status Quo, content, the goal is to focus on what you can ADD to their current situation that would move them closer to their objectives, NOT what you can REPLACE. Remember, even if they were not 100% content, or even 50%, they are not going to discuss that with an Interruption, that is why you are going for credibility. More importantly, they have been conditioned by all the sales people that they have dealt with in the past, a vast majority of whom have come with "get rid of what you have now, and replace it with my stuff". Frightening and costly. But if you can enhance what they have in place now, improve their investment in that, and more towards their goal, you have something that neutralizes their Conditioned Response and extends the conversation. Even for those buyers who are 100% satisfied with what they have in place, you could help them improve, enhance and go further.

A lot of people I call tell me they have in-house training, or are working with someone already. I also know that no program is complete, and usually could benefit from rounding out, so rather than knock up against what is already there, here is how I respond.

"I am glad you brought that up" (Acknowledge)
"XYZ Ltd., was in the same spot when we first called, but once they saw how our program was able to get their people in front of more prospects, they got to practice Wham Bam Consultative Selling they had in place with more buyers, generating more revenue and ROI on Wham Bam investment" (Credibility/Involve)
"Why don't I show how we did that, how is Wednesday at 11:00 for you?" (Call 2 Action)

The goal is to get the appointment with the prospect, not dislodge the incumbent, once you are "in the tent", you are in a different position.

With Lack of Interest, the focus is on value or benefit. The thinking is this, the main reason they are not interested is they haven't seen the value or benefit a meeting with you would bring. You have to be specific, not pie in the sky empty words they heard six times already this morning.

Identify where you have delivered tangible value to a similar company, to similar roles, the more similar the better. For example, I have done a lot of work in one specific industry, with a number of similar clients. This particular industry as a whole suffered from a high turnover of reps, which in turn had a knock-on negative impact on clients, revenues, and hiring related expenses. I learned that companies I worked with in the industry have been able to increase their retention of reps, and by extension client satisfaction, up-sell and retention, specifically because of my program. So when I call on others in similar scenarios, and they tell me they are not interested:

"I can see why you may feel that way, as the CFO at Red White and Blue initially had the same reaction" (Acknowledge)

"Until he saw how our program helped with increased revenue, reduce rep turnover cost, and improve client satisfaction" (Credibility/Involve)
"I can show exactly how we did that, how is Wednesday at 11:00?" (Call 2 Action)

Takes work, you have to understand what their priorities are, how your strengths align with their requirements and objectives, and other factors highlighted above, but the payoff is immediate and lasting, and your engagement rate will increase measurably.

www.SellBetter.ca

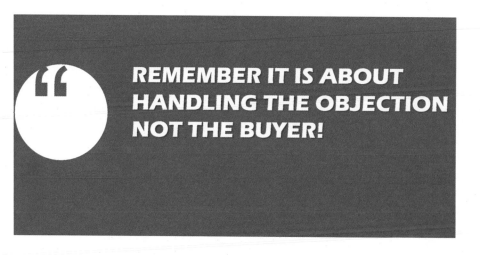

REMEMBER IT IS ABOUT HANDLING THE OBJECTION NOT THE BUYER!

CHAPTER FOUR

No Time

One of the easiest ways to dismiss Interruptions and to get the most out of Conditioned Responses, is by telling the caller that you are busy.

Prospect: I'm really busy, can you call me back?
Caller: Sure, when is a good time?
Prospect: Call me Tuesday morning!

Chick chack, the prospect is back to work in less than five seconds.

Let's look at the replay in slow motion.

First, notice how little effort was exerted by the Prospect, making full use of his Conditioned Response. Did you notice the head fake by the Prospect, deking out the Caller by offering false hope in feigning interest by asking the Caller to call back next Tuesday, as if there was a glimmer of hope; of course what he didn't bother telling the Caller is that he is off on vacation starting Monday.

A key reason it was so easy for the Prospect to deke out the Caller is that like most untrained cold callers they are more focused on getting off the phone than to completing the call successfully, given the opening by the Prospector, the Caller went for it with the most predictable and welcomed line.

Different Prospect: I'm sorry, but I am really busy right now
Caller: I just need a few minutes of your time
Different Prospect: Which part of busy now do I need to break down for you?
[click dial tone]

Prospects love the busy objection, it is the shortest line between ring and back to work. It sucks in the Caller by making them deal with the wrong element of the call, the focus should be on action, in the form of a meeting, not time.

That's right, the best way to deal with the busy Conditioned Response is to take the focus off time, and put it on action/outcome.

Prospect: Jim, I am really busy right now
Jim: I understand, in fact I thought you would be, (Acknowledge)
Jim: in fact I only work by appointment myself, which is the only reason for my call (Credibility, Involvement through curiosity); and the opportunity to differentiation yourself by the approach you bring.
Jim: can we do that Friday at 10:00? (Call to Action)

No fuss, no muss, just an effective way to deal with the prospect's Conditioned Response.

As with the other Conditioned Responses, be they Status Quo or Lack Of Interest, this paves the way for them responding to your Call to Action in the form of a time to meet, which in fact will be another objection, but this time no conditioned, but a direct response to you, and a start to a, rough, but nonetheless, a conversation. An opportunity for you to engage based factors relevant to the buyer.

THE BEST WAY TO DEAL WITH THE BUSY CONDITIONED RESPONSE IS TO TAKE THE FOCUS OFF TIME, AND PUT IT ON ACTION/OUTCOME

23

CHAPTER FIVE

Send Me Your Experience

Continuing our journey through the joys of Prospecting Rejection we arrive at two common objections, one my least favourite, the other which is probably not really so bad, but some sellers just take it the wrong way, and end up on the short end of the conversation.

My least favourite is the "send me some information" objection, not so much because it is hard to handle, but because I find them to be wimps, like Nancy said, "just say no"! Don't pretend to be interested just to get rid of someone, because if nothing else you are inviting another interruption when they call back to follow up on what ever they sent based on your request.

You could go to the extreme one company I know, where they make it a policy not to send, based on observation, this has not cost them opportunities. But let's take them at their word, and their statement at face value, specifically a level of interest. Rather than risking that interest, work to specify it. Highlight the fact that you have delivered many solutions to clients based on their situation, rather than send a lot of generic information, it has proven to be a better use of time to meet, specify, and leave behind the information that makes sense, and again end with a call to action.

With a bit of practice you can take this up a notch. Confirm that they are asking in order to better evaluate the need to meet, when they do, direct them to you web site, should be as practical as any brochure. If they are unwilling, you have saved time and effort. If they do, you can highlight the many aspects of your offering, continue to qualify, and move towards your goal with your call(s) to action.

One other thing you have to determine before you start, and that is what you will send. I stopped sending hard copies years ago, strictly e-mail, much more practical given the tools at hand these days. For me in the end I do send, as a VP once told me:

"Tibor it's like this, you send, you have a shot, you don't, we'll you don't"

Bad Experience

Not the send objection, but the objection that we all encounter. In many ways this is really not a rejection but an opportunity, but some sellers interpret it as one, and at times miss the opportunity.

In most instances people feel they had a bad a experience not because of what happened, but how it was resolved; more accurately not resolved in their view. We have all been to restaurants where the service or food was bad, but management took proactive steps to resolve things to the customer's satisfaction.

Face the issue head on, ask them to tell you exactly what happened, take interest, clearly no one did at the time things happened. Help them have a catharsis, until they rid themselves of the luggage they are carrying around, they will remained closed, so help them unload. Once they do, you'll have two opportunities, first they will see you as someone who was willing to listen to them; second, having relived them of their burden, you are in a position to offer a new alternative.

Word of caution, do not take ownership of whatever perceived issues they may have had. It is one thing to say you are sorry they felt that way, another to say "I am sorry that happened". The latter can be fatal as you are inadvertently acknowledging that it did happen the way they see it, and that you (your company) was responsible.

26

THERE SO MANY WAYS WE HELP, WHAT SPECIFCALLY ARE YOUR CURRENT OBJECTIVE?

CHAPTER SIX

The Non-Objection

In the first five chapters we looked at the nature of objections by potential prospects and how to best use them to transition an interruption to a conversation. But there is another side to objections that is common and needs to be dealt with in a different fashion - by getting ahead of it - what I call the Non-Objection. In case you are wondering this is no way related to the famous and perhaps mythical experimental Non-Rabbit.

The Non-Objection are those that can be avoided before they are ever presented; these will differ across industries, and will therefore require you to draw on your own experience to manage. Success with these objections rely on a basic tenant of sales success, specifically the **Three Rule**.

The Three Rule suggests that the first time you encounter something:

It is new and a surprise
The second time it is confirmation, and no longer a surprise
The third time it is our jobs as sales professionals to be ready and deal with it directly

Based on The Three Rule, it is up to me to anticipate and move to remove a potential objection from the equation. For example at the start of 2009, a number of people I was trying to engage with put up the recession as their reason for not wanting to engage with me, or trainers in general. Rather than changing professions, I changed my approach. In my introduction I included a variation of the following:

"I work with companies who have decided to take a proactive approach to selling in the recession."

This did not mean instant engagement, it certainly left the other common objections in play, but it took the recession "excuse", sorry, "objection", or Conditioned Response out of the mix, leveling the playing field.

Here is another example, I was working with a large international manufacturer, the team covering the SMB sector kept running into the same objection, especially with SOHO's, that "oh, we're too small dear". As a result we had them change their script and include statement:

"I am the small business specialist"

What was the prospect to say, "oh no, we are minuscule".

So if you are running into a specific objection other than the five we have prepped you for, step back and see how you can take it away before it is used against you. See how you can use it to your advantage by presenting it as a benefit, rather than have it used to weaken your position.

One other way to use The Non-Objection is in dealing with the Send objection. 90% of the time you call to follow up on a Send, you'll hear that they haven't had a chance to read it, or they have yet to get it. So when you follow up, start by saying:

"Harry, it's Tibor here, I am following up on our call last week and the information I sent as a result, YOU PROBABLY HAVEN'T HAD A CHANCE TO READ, HAVE YOU?"

Just the nervous laughter at the other end is worth the call alone. If they say no they hadn't, just say "that's exactly why I suggested we meet, how is Thursday at 10:00?"

30

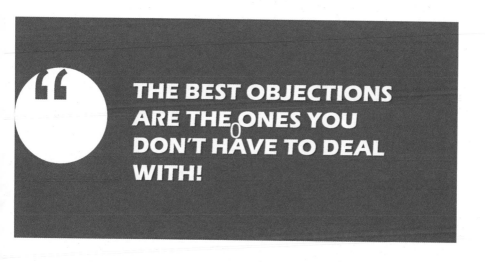

THE BEST OBJECTIONS ARE THE ONES YOU DON'T HAVE TO DEAL WITH!

31

About the author

Tibor Shanto

Tibor Shanto is recognized sales leader, the co-author of an award winning book on Trigger Event Selling, and Principal of Renbor Sales Solutions Inc. Tibor Delivers professional development for professional sales organizations. His work with leading B2B sales organizations such as Bell Mobility, Imperial Oil, Ricoh Canada and others, is focused on driving ongoing and sustainable behavioural change required to compete in today's demanding economy.

Called a brilliant sales tactician, Tibor works with companies to improve the execution of their process by helping translate sales strategy to tactical success. Focusing on key metrics, Tibor works with front line reps, line managers and senior leaders to drive results, including improved prospecting for new opportunities, shorter sales cycles, and consistent revenue and margin growth. When it comes to sales, Tibor understands that success comes from "Execution – Everything Else Is Just Talk!"

In addition to his books, Tibor is monthly contributor to The Globe and Mail's Report On Small Business, Office Technology Magazine, Today's Trucking and The Huffington Post. He has appeared on BNN, CHCH TV, Profit Magazine, and more. A prolific blogger, featured regularly on leading sales blogs including salesforce.com. As a speaker he has been featured at numerous events addressing sales and sales success with his unique view on how to sell better. Tibor is able to combine traditional selling with social selling, and was ranked 8th on the Top 30 Social Salespeople In The World – Forbes.com.

tibor.shanto@sellbetter.ca
+1 416 822-7781
(855) 25-SALES Toll Free

Tibor Shanto

 http://www.SellBetter.ca/Blog

http://twitter.com/TiborShanto

http://ca.linkedin.com/in/tiborshanto

http://www.youtube.com/sellbetter

http://gplus.to/TiborShanto

http://facebook.com/Renbor.Sellbetter

TIBOR SHANTO
AWARDS & RECOGNITION

- Ranked 8th on the Top 30 Social Salespeople In The World – Forbes.com 2014
- Top 50 Sales & Marketing Influencers for 2014 – Top Sales World
- Top 25 Sales Influencers for 2014– OpenView Labs
- Gold Medal Top Sales & Marketing Blog 2013 – Top Sales World Awards
- 50 Most Influential People in Sales Lead Management in 2013
- Top 50 Sales & Marketing Influencers for 2013 – Top Sales World
- Top 25 Sales Influencers for 2013– OpenView Labs
- 25 Influential Leaders In Sales – 2012 Edition – InsideView
- Top 50 Sales & Marketing Influencers for 2012 – Top Sales World
- Top 25 Sales Influencers for 2012 – OpenView Labs
- 50 Most Influential People in Sales Lead Management in 2010

Renbor Sales Solutions Inc. l 256 Thornway Ave Thornhill Ontario L4J 7X8 l info@sellbetter.ca l (855) 25-SALES

www.sellbetter.ca

Made in the USA
Columbia, SC
17 June 2022